Clouds and Waves

Rabindranath Tagore

Art by **Sunaina Coelho**

ॐ KATHA

"Come!
We play from the time we wake
till the day ends.
We play with the golden dawn
and the silver moon."

They answer,
"Come to the edge of the earth,
lift up your hands to the sky,
and you will be taken up
into the clouds."

"My Mother is waiting for me at home,"
I say, "how can I leave her and come?"
Then they smile and float away.

But I know
a nicer game than that, Mother.
I shall be the cloud and
you the moon.

The folk who live in the waves
call out to me ...
"Join in!
We sing from morning till night;
on and on we travel and
know not where we go."

They tell me,
"Come to the edge of the shore
and stand with your eyes tight shut,

and you will be carried out upon the waves."

But I know
a better game than that.

I will be the waves
and you will be a strange shore.
I shall roll on and on
and on
and break upon your lap
with laughter.

Rabindranath Tagore, lovingly called Gurudev, was born on May 7, 1861 in Calcutta. His father Debendranath Tagore was a Sanskrit scholar. Gurudev's early education was imparted at home. In school, while others use to learn their lessons, he would slip into more exciting world of dreams. He wrote his first poem when he was seven. At the age of seventeen, his first book of poems was published. His writings, with their magic and lyricism, stir deep emotions and makes one marvel at the ease of words and the flow with which he weaves them together. He was awarded the Nobel Prize in Literature in 1913 for his collection of well-known poems *Gitanjali*.

Sunaina Coelho studied animation at the National Institute of Design, Ahmedabad, and now lives in Mumbai where she does animation for Television. When she is not drawing, she is mostly sleeping, dreaming, cooking or sitting by the seaside, wishing it were clean enough to swim in.

Therefore Design was initiated by Vrishali Kekre, Nitin Virkar, Gauri Barve, Harini Chandrasekar and Dhun Patel — a diverse group of individuals who are passionate about design. Therefore Design is a multifaceted design house that offers services in Design Research, Communication Design and Industrial Design.

KATHA

First published © Katha, 2011
Copyright © Katha, 2011
Text copyright © Katha, 2011
Illustrations copyright © Rajiv Eipe, 2011
All rights reserved. No part of this book may be reproduced or utilized in any form without the prior written permission of the publisher.
Printed in New Delhi
ISBN 978-81-89934-83-5

KATHA is a registered nonprofit devoted to enhancing the joys of reading amongst children and adults. Katha Schools are situated in the slums and streets of Delhi and tribal villages of Arunachal Pradesh.
A3 Sarvodaya Enclave, Sri Aurobindo Marg
New Delhi 110 017
Phone: 4141 6600 . 4182 9998 . 2652 1752
Fax: 2651 4373
E-mail: marketing@katha.org, Website: www.katha.org

Ten per cent of sales proceeds from this book will support the quality education of children studying in Katha Schools.
Katha regularly plants trees to replace the wood used in the making of its books.
First Reprint 2013, Second Reprint 2015, Third Reprint 2017, Fourth Reprint 2019